To Chris   Christmas 2000

EDINBURGH

Colin Baxter Photography, Grantown-on-Spey, Scotland

EDINBURGH

Twentieth-century Edinburgh is internationally renowned for its Festival and Fringe; visitors from every corner of the world know well the contours of Arthur's Seat, the silhouette of the Castle and the pillared form of the unfinished replica of the Parthenon on Calton Hill.

The heart of Scotland's historic capital was a fortified medieval city. The main artery running through the 'Old Town', between the highest tenement buildings in Europe, is the famous Royal Mile. It leads from the Castle to the Palace of Holyrood and its Abbey, passing the crown steeple of St Giles' Cathedral and the old parliament building.

Edinburgh's 'New Town' is in complete contrast to the narrow streets and closes of the Old Town. Begun in 1767, the elegant Georgian townscape with its well proportioned buildings, crescents, wide streets and vistas, is the largest sequence of planned developments of its kind in Britain.

Of course, there is more: the famous Princes Street, flanked on one side by public gardens and dominated by the Castle; the many villages which were once separate settlements and now form characterful areas within the city; Leith with its docks and exciting new developments on the waterfront; and vibrant architecture from the late twentieth century, including the new conference centre and the Museum of Scotland. Edinburgh has all this and more, waiting to be discovered.

◀ THE CITY FROM
SALISBURY CRAGS

The first two syllables of 'Edinburgh'
probably come from the Gaelic *Din
Eidyn* meaning the 'fort on the hill'. The
hard basalt of Castle Rock offered that
original defensible site and Edinburgh
Castle still stands sentinel at the heart
of the city.

RAMSAY GARDEN ▶

Ramsay Garden on Castlehill, was
planned by Professor Patrick Geddes
as a university hall of residence, and
built in three stages between 1892 and
1894. It is largely Scots Baronial
architecture, but also incorporates an
earlier 18th-century octagonal house
which belonged to the poet Allan
Ramsay, father of the portrait painter.

◀ CHARLOTTE SQUARE

Edinburgh's classical 'New Town' had
several phases. The first was conceived
in grid plan by James Craig in 1766.
Construction began at the east end of
what became Princes Street, and moved
west. Charlotte Square, largely designed
by Robert Adam and completed in
1820, was the grand finale of the first
New Town.

THE CASTLE FROM
PRINCES STREET GARDENS ▶

The public gardens north of Princes
Street flourish where the Nor' Loch, a
defensive, artificial loch, was created in
1460. The loch was drained in 1820 when
West Princes Street Gardens were laid
out; they originally extended round Castle
Rock to the back of the Grassmarket.

◀ JOHN KNOX HOUSE, ROYAL MILE

The legend connecting John Knox, the protestant reformer, to this largely 16th-century house ensured its survival. Protruding into the High Street, part of the Royal Mile, the building may have begun as two storeys with a projecting stair. The third storey and front block was probably added by 1525.

ARTHUR'S SEAT ▶ AND SALISBURY CRAGS

Edinburgh's highest hill, Arthur's Seat at 823 ft (251 m) dominates the city. The remains of a volcano which erupted *c.*325 million years ago, its lava-formed slopes are interrupted by the ridge of Salisbury Crags; there are fine views of the city and beyond from the summit.

◄ EDINBURGH CASTLE AND THE
ROYAL MILE FROM THE AIR

The elongated 'Old Town' runs parallel
with the more recent Princes Street (on
left) and main Edinburgh railway line.
Scything through the jumble of streets
and maze of narrow closes, is the famous
Royal Mile. Dominated by tall tenements
it runs through the Old Town from the
Castle to Holyrood Palace.

Now highly attractive, in the 18th
century the area was crammed with
one and two-roomed homes, some
windowless, with no plumbing of any
kind. The street was an open sewer. By
the end of the century, when the first
'New Town' was home to 7000 in
roughly the equivalent area, the Old
Town contained 58,000 people, mostly
housed in tenements over 10 storeys high.

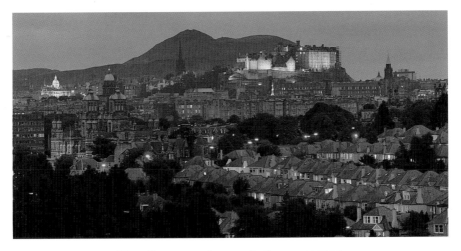

THE CITY AND ARTHUR'S SEAT AT DUSK

Illuminated against the dark silhouette of Arthur's Seat, Edinburgh Castle stands high on its basalt plinth. From fortress to royal residence, ordnance factory to home of Scotland's crown jewels, the present castle is the culmination of perhaps 7000 years of habitation, and forms a distinctive outline above both Old and New Towns.

◀ THE PALACE
OF HOLYROODHOUSE
AND HOLYROOD PARK

In the shadow of Arthur's Seat, on the
edge of Holyrood or the Queen's Park,
the turreted palace, dating from 1671-8,
is now the official residence of the
monarch in Scotland. It evolved from
the royal guesthouse once attached to the
now ruinous Abbey.

THE ROYAL MILE AND ▶
ST GILES' CATHEDRAL

St Giles' was a cathedral only for two
short periods, 1633-8 and 1661-89. Its
cathedral-like proportions and its location
mid-way down the High Street (on the
Royal Mile) reflect its role as the only
parish church in the burgh of Edinburgh
during the Middle Ages.

◄ GREYFRIARS' BOBBY

Bobby, the Skye terrier was immortalised
in bronze in 1872. Possibly a police
watchdog who remained in the area when
his master died, it is more popularly
believed that he lay on the grave of a
farmer, John Gray, for 14 years after he
died, turning up daily to be fed at nearby
John Traill's restaurant.

WEST BOW, GRASSMARKET ►
AND GEORGE HERIOT'S SCHOOL

Looking over the Grassmarket, formerly
a corn and livestock market, to George
Heriot's School. Goldsmith and money-
lender George Heriot (1563-1624),
'Jinglin' Geordie', bequeathed part of his
vast fortune to build a hospital for the care
and education of orphan boys. Today the
building is still in use as a private school.

THE CITY AT DUSK FROM CALTON HILL

RAMSAY GARDEN

The romantic red-roofed buildings of Ramsay Garden were designed in the 'organic and improvisatory' style of botanist and town planner Patrick Geddes. In 1887 he established the first student residence in Scotland on The Mound in Edinburgh and during the next decade built Ramsay Garden for the same purpose.

◀ EDINBURGH MILITARY TATTOO

Since 1950, three years after the first
'Edinburgh International Festival of
Music and Drama', the Tattoo has been
performed nightly during Festival-time on
the Castle Esplanade. With demonstrations
by international military forces, the
massed pipes and drums and the lone
piper spotlit on the Castle ramparts, the
Tattoo is a key Festival attraction.

VICTORIA STREET ▶

Surmounted on the north side by Victoria
Terrace, Victoria Street was built in 1827
to make a direct connection from the Old
Town to George IV Bridge. Down the
slope of the site, the buildings rise from
one to three storeys before butting onto
the earlier West Bow at the east end of
the Grassmarket.

◀ MELVILLE STREET

The detail of the New Town's ironwork, such as arched lampholders framing some of the entrances on Melville Street, adds considerably to its charm and formal design. The street was designed by Robert Brown in 1814, and offers one of the most impressive New Town vistas towards St Mary's Cathedral.

THE BALMORAL HOTEL, ▶
NORTH BRIDGE AND
CALTON HILL

The Balmoral Hotel (formerly the North British Hotel, 1902) dominates the east end of Princes Street at its junction with the North Bridge (1763-72). It was built to give access from the Old to the New Town, and renovated when Waverley Station was reconstructed in the 1980s.

THE FESTIVAL FRINGE OFFICE, ROYAL MILE

The Fringe emerged spontaneously alongside the first Festival in
1947 when eight theatre groups simply arrived to contribute.

◀ THE CITY FROM CALTON HILL

EDINBURGH CASTLE AND CITY AT SUNSET

Silhouetted against the setting sun: from left to right, the three spires of St Mary's Cathedral, the prominent mass of the Castle and the single spire of the Tolbooth Church, which was designed with fine Gothic detail in 1839-44.

ST GILES' CATHEDRAL ▶ AND ROYAL MILE

More correctly, 'the High Kirk of Edinburgh', St Giles' dominates the Royal Mile at Parliament Square. The earliest features are four Norman columns which support the lantern or crown, itself surmounted by a golden weathercock (1567). The medieval church is hidden behind an early 19th-century renovation which left only the central crown-tower untouched. Until then, the façade was largely obscured by the Old Tolbooth and luckenbooths (lock-up stalls). The tall tapering 1828 steeple beyond St Giles' is a feature of the reconstructed Tron Church, originally built in 1636-47 for St Giles' congregation when it temporarily held cathedral status.

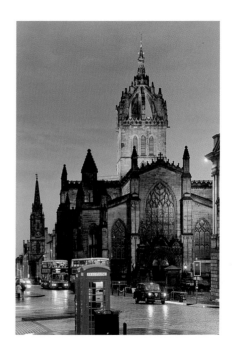

◄ EDINBURGH CASTLE AND RAMSAY GARDEN

Today the castle and highly desirable Ramsay Garden look out over the lush green of Princes Street Gardens. At the beginning of the 18th century the same view was of the evil-smelling Nor', or North Loch, its condition in no small part due to the slaughtermen, skinners and tanners who worked around it.

WHITEHORSE CLOSE ►

Possibly the most pleasing of Edinburgh's closes, Whitehorse Close has been described as 'a Hollywood dream of the 17th century'. It was originally built towards the end of that century but was reconstructed after 1889 and again in 1962 when traditional harling was employed to cover modern brickwork.

◀ Moray Place
and Ainslie Place,
New Town, from the air

The 'foliaged compartments' of the Moray
Estate are the most geometrically complex
of all the New Town areas. Designed by
James Gillespie Graham in 1822, the area
cleverly dovetails into the First, Northern,
and later Western New Town.

New Town Door ▶

Edinburgh's New Town is an architectural
gem, the world's largest Georgian
development and probably the most
perfect. Covering about 1 square mile, it
contains over 11,000 properties. In 1799,
32 years after it was begun, grass still
grew in almost every street because, in
marked contrast to the Old Town,
pressure of population was low.

◄ PRINCES STREET AT DUSK

Part of the first phase of the New Town, Princes Street was planned as single-sided and residential with panoramic views of the Old Town and castle over Princes Street Gardens. Although many of the original houses survive, by the end of the 19th century it was becoming more the shopping street it is today.

THE OLD TOWN ►
AND ST GILES' CATHEDRAL

The apparently chaotic northern façade of Edinburgh's Old Town cascades down a steep slope. In the 16th century the Old Town housed 700 people to the acre and Edinburgh was the most over-crowded city in Europe. The tenements graded society vertically; the more genteel living on the upper floors.

EDINBURGH CASTLE AND THE CITY AT TWILIGHT

Published in Great Britain in 1999 by Colin Baxter Photography Ltd,
Grantown-on-Spey, Moray PH26 3NA, Scotland

Text by Lorna Ewan

A CIP Catalogue record for this book is available from the British Library.

ISBN 1-84107-007-6   *Colin Baxter Gift Book Series*   Printed in Hong Kong

Page one photograph: **Chimneys, Old Town**   Page two photograph: **Edinburgh Castle and Princes Street Gardens**
Front cover photograph: **Edinburgh Castle and Old Town**   Back cover photograph: **Old Town Rooftops and Spires**